DINOSAUR WORLD

Lizard Tooth
The Adventure of Iguanadon

Written by Michael Dahl

Illustrated by Garry Nichols

Special thanks to our advisers for their expertise:

Philip J. Currie, Curator of Dinosaurs,
Royal Tyrrell Museum of Palaeontology, Drumheller, Alberta, Canada

Susan Kesselring, M.A., Literacy Educator,
Rosemount - Apple Valley - Eagan (Minnesota) School District

PICTURE WINDOW BOOKS
Minneapolis, Minnesota

Managing Editor: Catherine Neitge
Creative Director: Terri Foley
Art Director: Keith Griffin
Editor: Patricia Stockland
Designer: Joe Anderson
Page production: Picture Window Books
The illustrations in this book were prepared digitally.

Picture Window Books
5115 Excelsior Boulevard
Suite 232
Minneapolis, MN 55416
877-845-8392
www.picturewindowbooks.com

Printed in the United States of America.

Library of Congress Cataloging-in-Publication Data
Dahl, Michael.
Lizard tooth : the adventure of Iguanodon / written by
Michael Dahl ; illustrated by Garry Nichols.
p. cm. — (Dinosaur world)
Includes bibliographical references and index.
ISBN 1-4048-0942-2 (hardcover)
1. Iguanodon—Juvenile literature. I. Nichols, Garry, 1958-
ill. II. Title.

QE862.O65D32 2005
567.914—dc22
                                   2004018519

No humans lived during the time of the dinosaurs. No person heard them roar, saw their scales, or felt their feathers.

The giant creatures are gone, but their fossils, or remains, lie hidden in the earth. Dinosaur skulls, skeletons, and eggs have been buried in rock for millions of years.

All around the world, scientists dig up fossils and carefully study them. Bones show how tall the dinosaurs stood. Claws and teeth show how they grabbed and what they ate. Scientists compare fossils with the bodies of living creatures such as birds and reptiles, which are relatives of the dinosaurs. Every year, scientists learn more and more about the giants that have disappeared.

Studying fossils and figuring out how the dinosaurs lived is like putting together the pieces of a puzzle that is millions of years old.

This is what some of those pieces can tell us about the dinosaur known as *Iguanodon* (i-GWA-no-dan).

A fiery sun blazed in the sky. The air was warm. The trees were still. The afternoon grew hotter and hotter.

Iguanodon walked slowly across the plain. Each heavy step raised a cloud of dust.

Iguanodon was as tall as an elephant, but its body and tail were much longer. An adult *Iguanodon* was a little bigger than a military tank.

Iguanodon traveled on four powerful legs. Clomp! Clomp! The strong feet plodded on the dry ground. *Iguanodon*'s toes ended in flat, blunt claws. The hoof-like claws dug into the dirt as *Iguanodon* wandered across the plain, looking for leaves to eat.

Scientists have found footprints left by *Iguanodon*. The prints reveal that *Iguanodon* often walked on its thick toes, like dogs and cats. The nails on the ends of *Iguanodon*'s front middle toes were like small hooves.

A hot breeze blew across the ground. *Iguanodon* stopped and lifted its head. Far away, dark clouds were gathering.

Iguanodon smelled a welcome scent in the air.
Rain was coming.

Iguanodon lived about 125 million years ago, during the Early Cretaceous period. At that time, most of Earth had the same climate. The climate was good for growing lots of plants.

9

Iguanodon found a small tree. The green leaves fluttered in the breeze. Iguanodon stripped the branches bare with its beak.

Iguanodon was an herbivore, a plant-eating dinosaur. Its toothless beak was good for ripping leaves off tree branches. Rows of strong teeth lined the jaws of *Iguanodon*'s mouth. These side teeth were used for grinding and shredding the creature's leafy meals. *Iguanodon* means "iguana tooth." Its teeth look like the teeth of an iguana, a modern-day lizard.

11

At the top of the tree, a few leaves still fluttered. *Iguanodon* grasped the tree with one of its front feet. Snap! The leaves disappeared between the dinosaur's jaws.

Iguanodon was able to stand or run on its powerful hind legs. The plant-eater was one of the few dinosaurs that could easily move on two or four legs. On each hand, *Iguanodon* had a bony thumb that looked like a sharp thorn or spike. The spike was as long as a human hand. Some scientists think *Iguanodon* used the spike as a weapon, or to hold its food.

13

Iguanodon was thirsty, but there were no streams or lakes nearby. A long hot spell had dried up all the drinking water on the plain. *Iguanodon* and its cousins had not drunk fresh water for several days.

Scientists believe that *Iguanodon* was a herd animal. Bone beds are places where many dinosaur fossils are found together in a heap. In some areas, scientists have found up to 30 *Iguanodon* skeletons lying together. Some scientists think that the dinosaurs traveled and fed together in large family groups.

Iguanodon stared up and blinked. The air still felt hot. Dark clouds now filled the sky.

Crack! Lightning flashed. Thunder boomed. Strong winds blew across the plains and shook the trees. The rain came down.

Iguanodon thumped back down on all four feet. Its long, stiff tail swung out and helped *Iguanodon* turn around swiftly. The dinosaur moved across the ground, heading back toward the herd.

Iguanodon was fast. With its strong leg muscles and streamlined body, *Iguanodon* was probably a good runner.

17

Sheets of rain poured from the sky. *Iguanodon* hunkered down against the ground. Streams of water rolled off its tough, thick skin.

As the dry dirt turned into mud beneath *Iguanodon*'s toes, small streams and pools formed on the ground.

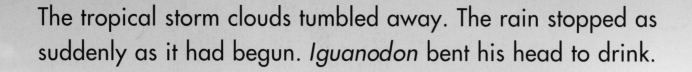

The tropical storm clouds tumbled away. The rain stopped as suddenly as it had begun. *Iguanodon* bent his head to drink.

Iguanodon: Where ...

Iguanodon fossils have been found around the world: North Africa, Europe, and England, as well as the United States in Utah and South Dakota.

... and When

The "Age of Dinosaurs" began 248 million years ago (mya). If we imagine the time from the beginning of the dinosaur age to the present as one day, the Age of Dinosaurs lasted 18 hours—and humans have only been around for 10 minutes!

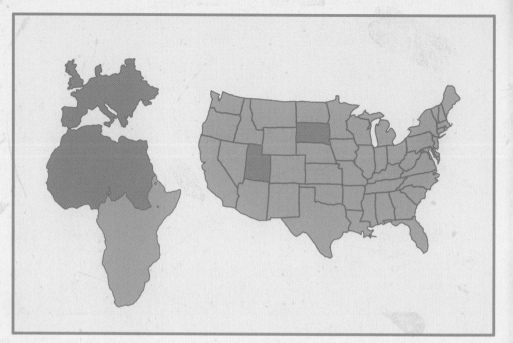

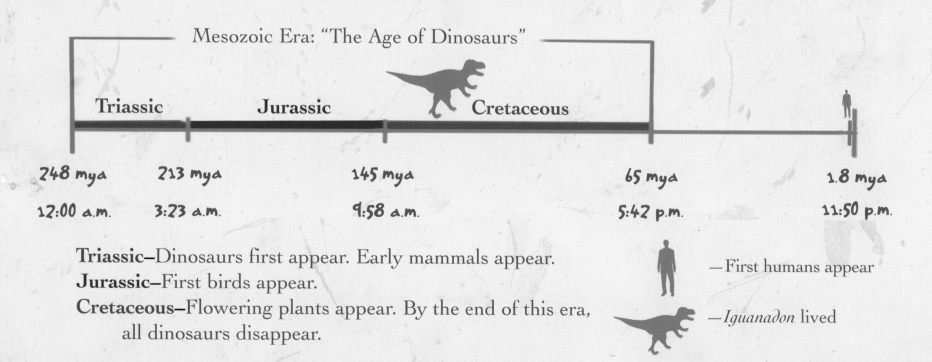

Mesozoic Era: "The Age of Dinosaurs"

Triassic   Jurassic   Cretaceous

248 mya	213 mya	145 mya	65 mya	1.8 mya
12:00 a.m.	3:23 a.m.	9:58 a.m.	5:42 p.m.	11:50 p.m.

Triassic—Dinosaurs first appear. Early mammals appear.
Jurassic—First birds appear.
Cretaceous—Flowering plants appear. By the end of this era, all dinosaurs disappear.

—First humans appear

—*Iguanadon* lived

Digging Deeper

Famous First

The first dinosaur fossil ever found belonged to *Iguanodon*. In 1822, Dr. Gideon Mantell, an amateur geologist, discovered large teeth buried in a forest in southern England. The teeth looked like the teeth of a modern-day iguana, except they were much larger. Mantell figured the teeth came from a previously undiscovered creature. He named the creature *Iguanodon*. Five of the original discovered teeth are still in the Natural History Museum of London, England.

Nose or Not?

Scientists sometimes make mistakes. When Dr. Mantell dug up an *Iguanodon* spike fossil, it reminded him of a rhinoceros horn. It also looked like the nose-horn on some modern iguanas. So when the first dinosaur drawings were made and the first dinosaur models were put together, scientists put the spike on *Iguanodon's* nose.

Thumbs Up

Fifty years after Dr. Mantell's discovery, coalmine workers in Bernissart, Belgium, found similar fossils in one large site. They eventually dug up 31 complete fossil skeletons! All the fossils belonged to *Iguanodon*. These skeletons showed where the bony spikes really went—on the dinosaur's thumbs.

Snack Track

A trackway is the name scientists give to a set of dinosaur footprints preserved in rock. One of the longest and best-preserved trackways is found in southern England. The prints were made by *Iguanodon*. Recently, some scientists have noticed another set of footprints near the same trackway. These new prints were made by *Megolosaurus*, a massive meat-eater who may have been following *Iguanodon*, hoping for a meal.

Words to Know

dinosaurs—giant creatures that lived millions of years ago; scientists think that many modern reptiles and birds are related to dinosaurs

herbivore—a creature that eats only plants

iguana—modern-day lizard with small, sharp teeth

streamlined—smooth or fast

trackway—a set of dinosaur tracks preserved in rock

To Learn More

At the Library

Cohen, Daniel. *Iguanodon.* Mankato, Minn.: Bridgestone Books, 2003.

Gray, Susan H. *Iguanodon.* Chanhassen, Minn.: Child's World, 2004.

Hartzog, Brooke. *Iguanodon and Dr. Gideon Mantell.* New York: PowerKids Press, 1999.

Rodriguez, K.S. *Iguanodon.* Austin, Tex.: Steadwell Books, 2000.

On the Web

FactHound offers a safe, fun way to find Web sites related to this book. All of the sites on FactHound have been researched by our staff. *www.facthound.com*

1. Visit the FactHound home page.
2. Enter a search word related to this book, or type in this special code: 1404809422
3. Click on the FETCH IT button.

Your trusty FactHound will fetch the best Web sites for you!